Table of Contents

This Notebook Belongs To

DoodleArts.com

Birthday Reminder

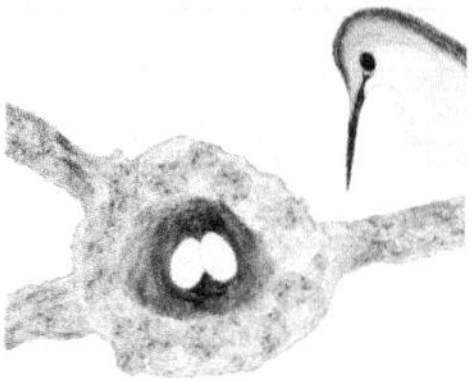

January	February	March

April	May	June

July	August	September

October	November	December

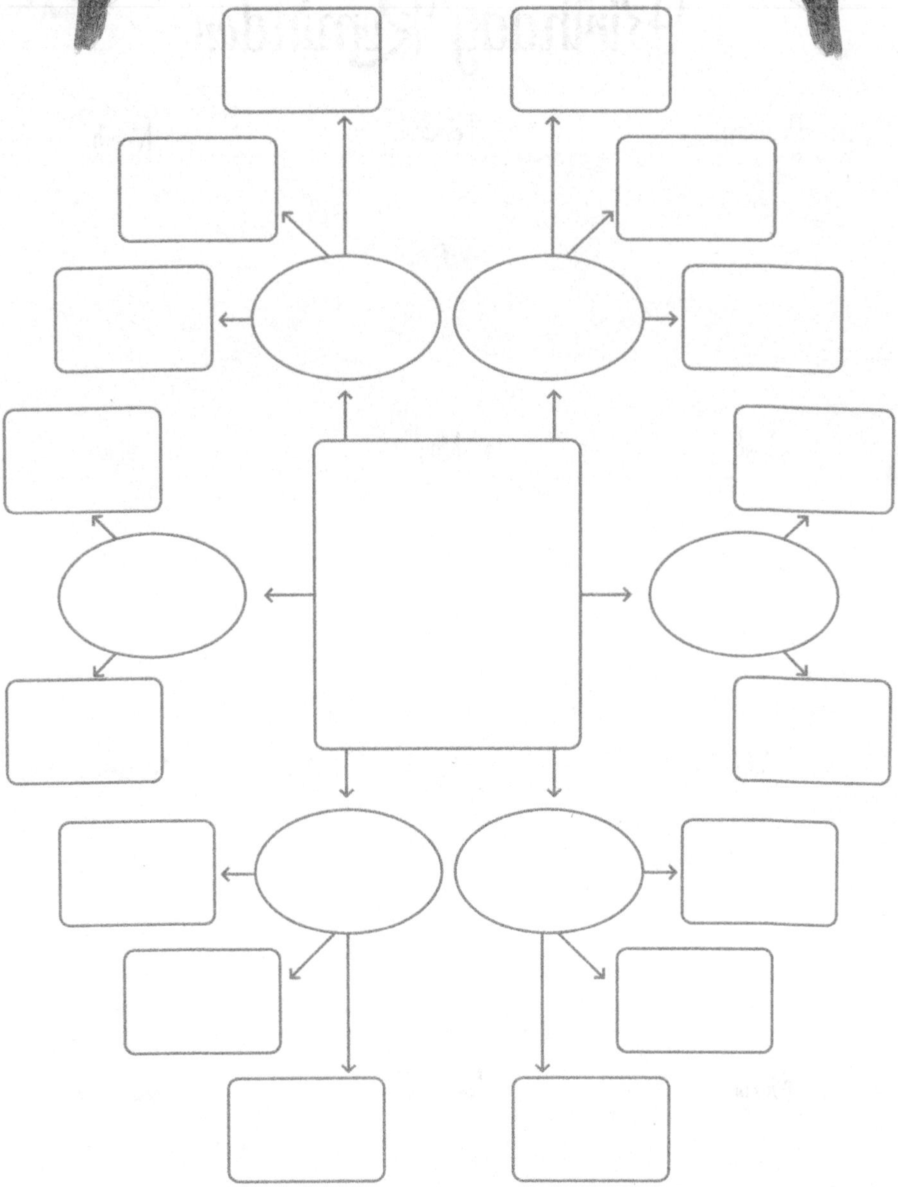

CAREER PLAN

PLAN PERIOD

CURRENT POSITION

GOALS

SHORT TERM GOALS

MID TERM GOALS

LONG TERM GOALS

HOW I'LL MAKE IT HAPPEN

CURRENT SKILLS EXPERIENCE KNOWLEDGE

NEW SKILLS EXPERIENCE KNOWLEDGE REQUIRED

MONTHLY TO-DO LIST

JANUARY	FEBRUARY	MARCH
APRIL	MAY	JUNE
JULY	AUGUST	SEPTEMBER
OCTOBER	NOVEMBER	DECEMBER

DAY PLANNER

Date: ____________

M T W Th F Sa Su

To Do

Priorities

Enthusiastic for

Appointments

Breakfast

Lunch

Dinner

Snack

Fitness

Mood

DAY PLANNER

Date:

M T W Th F Sa Su

To Do

Priorities

Enthusiastic for

Appointments

Breakfast

Lunch

Dinner

Snack

Fitness

Mood

DAY PLANNER

Date:

M T W Th F Sa Su

To Do

Priorities

Enthusiastic for

Appointments

Breakfast

Lunch

Dinner

Snack

Fitness

Mood

DAY PLANNER

Date:

M T W Th F Sa Su

Priorities

To Do

Enthusiastic for

Appointments

Breakfast	Lunch	Dinner	Snack

Fitness	Mood

DAY PLANNER

Date:

M T W Th F Sa Su

To Do

Priorities

Enthusiastic for

Appointments

Breakfast

Lunch

Dinner

Snack

Fitness

Mood

DAY PLANNER

Date:

M T W Th F Sa Su

To Do

Priorities

Enthusiastic for

Appointments

Breakfast

Lunch

Dinner

Snack

Fitness

Mood

DAY PLANNER

Date:

M T W Th F Sa Su

To Do

Priorities

Enthusiastic for

Appointments

Breakfast

Lunch

Dinner

Snack

Fitness

Mood

DAY PLANNER

Date: ____________

M T W Th F Sa Su

To Do

Priorities

Enthusiastic for

Appointments

Breakfast

Lunch

Dinner

Snack

Fitness

Mood

DAY PLANNER

Date: ____________

M T W Th F Sa Su

To Do

Priorities

Enthusiastic for

Appointments

Breakfast

Lunch

Dinner

Snack

Fitness

Mood

DAY PLANNER

Date:

M T W Th F Sa Su

To Do

Priorities

Enthusiastic for

Appointments

Breakfast

Lunch

Dinner

Snack

Fitness

Mood

DAY PLANNER

Date:

M T W Th F Sa Su

Priorities

To Do

Enthusiastic for

Appointments

Breakfast

Lunch

Dinner

Snack

Fitness

Mood

DAY PLANNER

Date:

M T W Th F Sa Su

To Do

Priorities

Enthusiastic for

Appointments

Breakfast

Lunch

Dinner

Snack

Fitness

Mood

DAY PLANNER

Date:

M T W Th F Sa Su

To Do

Priorities

Enthusiastic for

Appointments

Breakfast

Lunch

Dinner

Snack

Fitness

Mood

DAY PLANNER

Date:

M T W Th F Sa Su

To Do

Priorities

Enthusiastic for

Appointments

Breakfast

Lunch

Dinner

Snack

Fitness

Mood

DAY PLANNER

Date:

M T W Th F Sa Su

To Do

Priorities

Enthusiastic for

Appointments

Breakfast

Lunch

Dinner

Snack

Fitness

Mood

DAY PLANNER

Date:

M T W Th F Sa Su

To Do

Priorities

Enthusiastic for

Appointments

Breakfast

Lunch

Dinner

Snack

Fitness

Mood

DAY PLANNER

Date: ____________

M T W Th F Sa Su

To Do

Priorities

Enthusiastic for

Appointments

Breakfast

Lunch

Dinner

Snack

Fitness

Mood

DAY PLANNER

Date: ____________

M T W Th F Sa Su

To Do

Priorities

Enthusiastic for

Appointments

Breakfast

Lunch

Dinner

Snack

Fitness

Mood

DAY PLANNER

Date:

M T W Th F Sa Su

To Do

Priorities

Enthusiastic for

Appointments

Breakfast

Lunch

Dinner

Snack

Fitness

Mood

DAY PLANNER

Date:

M T W Th F Sa Su

To Do

Priorities

Enthusiastic for

Appointments

Breakfast

Lunch

Dinner

Snack

Fitness

Mood

DAY PLANNER

Date:

M T W Th F Sa Su

To Do

Priorities

Enthusiastic for

Appointments

Breakfast

Lunch

Dinner

Snack

Fitness

Mood

DAY PLANNER

Date:

M T W Th F Sa Su

Priorities

To Do

Enthusiastic for

Appointments

Breakfast

Lunch

Dinner

Snack

Fitness

Mood

DAY PLANNER

Date:

M T W Th F Sa Su

To Do

Priorities

Enthusiastic for

Appointments

Breakfast

Lunch

Dinner

Snack

Fitness

Mood

DAY PLANNER

Date:

M T W Th F Sa Su

To Do

Priorities

Enthusiastic for

Appointments

Breakfast

Lunch

Dinner

Snack

Fitness

Mood

DAY PLANNER

Date:

M T W Th F Sa Su

To Do

Priorities

Enthusiastic for

Appointments

Breakfast

Lunch

Dinner

Snack

Fitness

Mood

DAY PLANNER

Date: ____________

M T W Th F Sa Su

Priorities

To Do

Enthusiastic for

Appointments

Breakfast

Lunch

Dinner

Snack

Fitness

Mood

DAY PLANNER

Date:

M T W Th F Sa Su

To Do

Priorities

Enthusiastic for

Appointments

Breakfast

Lunch

Dinner

Snack

Fitness

Mood

DAY PLANNER

Date:

M T W Th F Sa Su

To Do

Priorities

Enthusiastic for

Appointments

Breakfast

Lunch

Dinner

Snack

Fitness

Mood

DAY PLANNER

Date:

M T W Th F Sa Su

To Do

Priorities

Enthusiastic for

Appointments

Breakfast

Lunch

Dinner

Snack

Fitness

Mood

DAY PLANNER

Date:

M T W Th F Sa Su

To Do

Priorities

Enthusiastic for

Appointments

Breakfast

Lunch

Dinner

Snack

Fitness

Mood

DAY PLANNER

Date:

M T W Th F Sa Su

To Do

Priorities

Enthusiastic for

Appointments

Breakfast

Lunch

Dinner

Snack

Fitness

Mood

DAY PLANNER

Date:

M T W Th F Sa Su

Priorities

To Do

Enthusiastic for

Appointments

Breakfast	Lunch	Dinner	Snack

Fitness	Mood

DAY PLANNER

Date:

M T W Th F Sa Su

To Do

Priorities

Enthusiastic for

Appointments

Breakfast

Lunch

Dinner

Snack

Fitness

Mood

DAY PLANNER

Date:

M T W Th F Sa Su

To Do

Priorities

Enthusiastic for

Appointments

Breakfast

Lunch

Dinner

Snack

Fitness

Mood

DAY PLANNER

Date:

M T W Th F Sa Su

To Do

Priorities

Enthusiastic for

Appointments

Breakfast

Lunch

Dinner

Snack

Fitness

Mood

DAY PLANNER

Date:

M T W Th F Sa Su

To Do

Priorities

Enthusiastic for

Appointments

Breakfast

Lunch

Dinner

Snack

Fitness

Mood

DAY PLANNER

Date:

M T W Th F Sa Su

To Do

Priorities

Enthusiastic for

Appointments

Breakfast

Lunch

Dinner

Snack

Fitness

Mood

DAY PLANNER

Date:

M T W Th F Sa Su

To Do

Priorities

Enthusiastic for

Appointments

Breakfast

Lunch

Dinner

Snack

Fitness

Mood

DAY PLANNER

Date:

M T W Th F Sa Su

To Do

Priorities

Enthusiastic for

Appointments

Breakfast

Lunch

Dinner

Snack

Fitness

Mood

DAY PLANNER

Date:

M T W Th F Sa Su

To Do

Priorities

Enthusiastic for

Appointments

Breakfast

Lunch

Dinner

Snack

Fitness

Mood

DAY PLANNER

Date:

M T W Th F Sa Su

To Do

Priorities

Enthusiastic for

Appointments

Breakfast

Lunch

Dinner

Snack

Fitness

Mood

DAY PLANNER

Date:

M T W Th F Sa Su

To Do

Priorities

Enthusiastic for

Appointments

Breakfast

Lunch

Dinner

Snack

Fitness

Mood

DAY PLANNER

Date:

M T W Th F Sa Su

To Do

Priorities

Enthusiastic for

Appointments

Breakfast

Lunch

Dinner

Snack

Fitness

Mood

DAY PLANNER

Date: ______

M T W Th F Sa Su

To Do

Priorities

Enthusiastic for

Appointments

Breakfast

Lunch

Dinner

Snack

Fitness

Mood

DAY PLANNER

Date: ________

M T W Th F Sa Su

To Do

Priorities

Enthusiastic for

Appointments

Breakfast

Lunch

Dinner

Snack

Fitness

Mood

DAY PLANNER

Date:

M T W Th F Sa Su

To Do

Priorities

Enthusiastic for

Appointments

Breakfast

Lunch

Dinner

Snack

Fitness

Mood

DAY PLANNER

Date:

M T W Th F Sa Su

To Do

Priorities

Enthusiastic for

Appointments

Breakfast

Lunch

Dinner

Snack

Fitness

Mood

DAY PLANNER

Date:

M T W Th F Sa Su

To Do

Priorities

Enthusiastic for

Appointments

Breakfast

Lunch

Dinner

Snack

Fitness

Mood

DAY PLANNER

Date:

M T W Th F Sa Su

To Do

Priorities

Enthusiastic for

Appointments

Breakfast

Lunch

Dinner

Snack

Fitness

Mood

DAY PLANNER

Date:

M T W Th F Sa Su

To Do

Priorities

Enthusiastic for

Appointments

Breakfast

Lunch

Dinner

Snack

Fitness

Mood

DAY PLANNER

Date:

M T W Th F Sa Su

To Do

Priorities

Enthusiastic for

Appointments

Breakfast

Lunch

Dinner

Snack

Fitness

Mood

DAY PLANNER

Date:

M T W Th F Sa Su

To Do

Priorities

Enthusiastic for

Appointments

Breakfast

Lunch

Dinner

Snack

Fitness

Mood

Weekly Meal Planner

Monday

Tuesday

Wednesday

Thursday

Friday

Saturday

Sunday

Shopping List

- [ ]
- [ ]
- [ ]
- [ ]
- [ ]
- [ ]
- [ ]
- [ ]
- [ ]
- [ ]
- [ ]
- [ ]
- [ ]
- [ ]
- [ ]
- [ ]
- [ ]
- [ ]
- [ ]
- [ ]
- [ ]
- [ ]
- [ ]
- [ ]
- [ ]
- [ ]
- [ ]
- [ ]
- [ ]
- [ ]
- [ ]

Weekly Meal Planner

Monday

Tuesday

Wednesday

Thursday

Friday

Saturday

Sunday

Shopping List

- [ ]
- [ ]
- [ ]
- [ ]
- [ ]
- [ ]
- [ ]
- [ ]
- [ ]
- [ ]
- [ ]
- [ ]
- [ ]
- [ ]
- [ ]
- [ ]
- [ ]
- [ ]
- [ ]
- [ ]
- [ ]
- [ ]
- [ ]
- [ ]
- [ ]
- [ ]
- [ ]
- [ ]
- [ ]
- [ ]

Weekly Meal Planner

Monday

Tuesday

Wednesday

Thursday

Friday

Saturday

Sunday

Shopping List

Weekly Meal Planner

Monday

Tuesday

Wednesday

Thursday

Friday

Saturday

Sunday

Shopping List

- [ ]
- [ ]
- [ ]
- [ ]
- [ ]
- [ ]
- [ ]
- [ ]
- [ ]
- [ ]
- [ ]
- [ ]
- [ ]
- [ ]
- [ ]
- [ ]
- [ ]
- [ ]
- [ ]
- [ ]
- [ ]
- [ ]
- [ ]
- [ ]
- [ ]
- [ ]
- [ ]
- [ ]
- [ ]
- [ ]
- [ ]

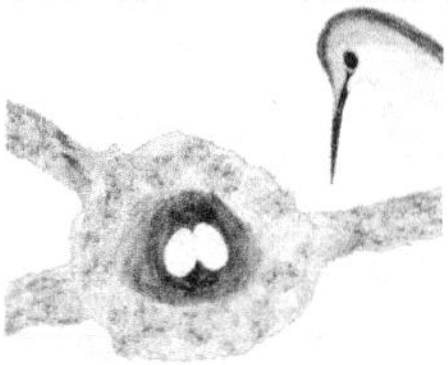

Project to complete

project

deadline

completed ☐

items required

tasks to-do

project

deadline

completed ☐

items required

tasks to-do

Project to complete

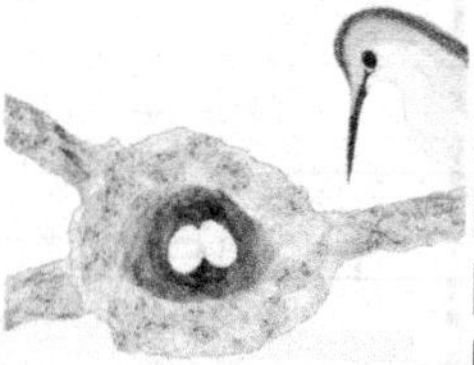

project

deadline

completed ☐

items required

tasks to-do

project

deadline

completed ☐

items required

tasks to-do

Project to complete

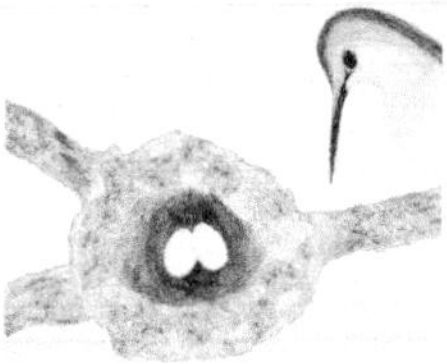

project	
deadline	completed ☐

items required

tasks to-do

project	
deadline	completed ☐

items required

tasks to-do

WORKOUT LOG

NAME:________________________ GOALS:________________________

EXERCISES	SETS	REPS	WT	REST	TIME	1RM	NOTES

DATE:________ WEIGHT:________ SLEEP:________ CALORIES:________

EXERCISES	SETS	REPS	WT	REST	TIME	1RM	NOTES

DATE:________ WEIGHT:________ SLEEP:________ CALORIES:________

EXERCISES	SETS	REPS	WT	REST	TIME	1RM	NOTES

DATE:________ WEIGHT:________ SLEEP:________ CALORIES:________

EXERCISES	SETS	REPS	WT	REST	TIME	1RM	NOTES

DATE:________ WEIGHT:________ SLEEP:________ CALORIES:________

EXERCISES	SETS	REPS	WT	REST	TIME	1RM	NOTES

DATE:________ WEIGHT:________ SLEEP:________ CALORIES:________

WORKOUT LOG

NAME:______________________ GOALS:____________________

EXERCISES	SETS	REPS	WT	REST	TIME	1RM	NOTES

DATE:_______ WEIGHT:_______ SLEEP:_______ CALORIES:_______

EXERCISES	SETS	REPS	WT	REST	TIME	1RM	NOTES

DATE:_______ WEIGHT:_______ SLEEP:_______ CALORIES:_______

EXERCISES	SETS	REPS	WT	REST	TIME	1RM	NOTES

DATE:_______ WEIGHT:_______ SLEEP:_______ CALORIES:_______

EXERCISES	SETS	REPS	WT	REST	TIME	1RM	NOTES

DATE:_______ WEIGHT:_______ SLEEP:_______ CALORIES:_______

EXERCISES	SETS	REPS	WT	REST	TIME	1RM	NOTES

DATE:_______ WEIGHT:_______ SLEEP:_______ CALORIES:_______

WORKOUT LOG

NAME:____________________ GOALS:____________________

EXERCISES	SETS	REPS	WT	REST	TIME	1RM	NOTES

DATE:________ WEIGHT:________ SLEEP:________ CALORIES:________

EXERCISES	SETS	REPS	WT	REST	TIME	1RM	NOTES

DATE:________ WEIGHT:________ SLEEP:________ CALORIES:________

EXERCISES	SETS	REPS	WT	REST	TIME	1RM	NOTES

DATE:________ WEIGHT:________ SLEEP:________ CALORIES:________

EXERCISES	SETS	REPS	WT	REST	TIME	1RM	NOTES

DATE:________ WEIGHT:________ SLEEP:________ CALORIES:________

EXERCISES	SETS	REPS	WT	REST	TIME	1RM	NOTES

DATE:________ WEIGHT:________ SLEEP:________ CALORIES:________

WORKOUT LOG

NAME:______________________ GOALS:____________________

EXERCISES	SETS	REPS	WT	REST	TIME	1RM	NOTES

DATE:_________ WEIGHT:_________ SLEEP:_________ CALORIES:_________

EXERCISES	SETS	REPS	WT	REST	TIME	1RM	NOTES

DATE:_________ WEIGHT:_________ SLEEP:_________ CALORIES:_________

EXERCISES	SETS	REPS	WT	REST	TIME	1RM	NOTES

DATE:_________ WEIGHT:_________ SLEEP:_________ CALORIES:_________

EXERCISES	SETS	REPS	WT	REST	TIME	1RM	NOTES

DATE:_________ WEIGHT:_________ SLEEP:_________ CALORIES:_________

EXERCISES	SETS	REPS	WT	REST	TIME	1RM	NOTES

DATE:_________ WEIGHT:_________ SLEEP:_________ CALORIES:_________

RUNNING / JOGGING LOG

YEAR ______ MONTH ______

DATE	DISTANCE	TIME	PACE	HR	REST HR	RUN TYPE	SHOES	NOTES

RUNNING / JOGGING LOG

YEAR ______ MONTH ______

DATE	DISTANCE	TIME	PACE	HR	REST HR	RUN TYPE	SHOES	NOTES

RUNNING / JOGGING LOG

YEAR ______ MONTH ______

DATE	DISTANCE	TIME	PACE	HR	REST HR	RUN TYPE	SHOES	NOTES

RUNNING / JOGGING LOG

YEAR ______ MONTH ______

DATE	DISTANCE	TIME	PACE	HR	REST HR	RUN TYPE	SHOES	NOTES

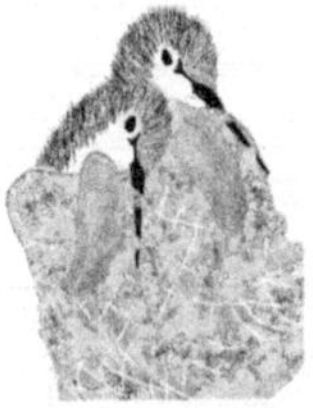

- Self Care -

This Week's Motto____

____

Self-Care Practices	Mon	Tue	Wed	Thu	Fri	Sat	Sun

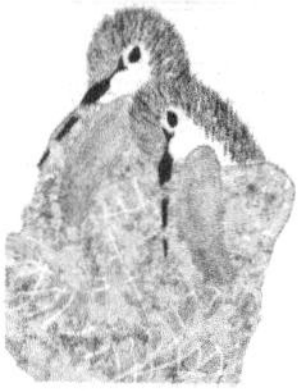

- Self Care -

This Week's Motto____

____

Self-Care Practices	Mon	Tue	Wed	Thu	Fri	Sat	Sun

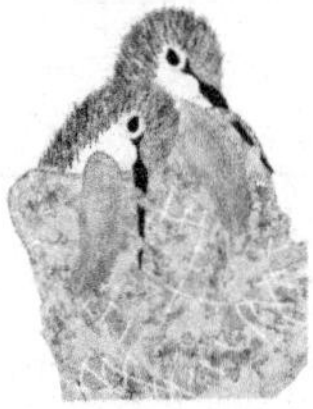

- Self Care -

This Week's Motto____

____

Self-Care Practices	Mon	Tue	Wed	Thu	Fri	Sat	Sun

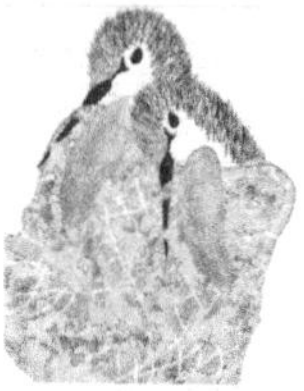

- Self Care -

This Week's Motto____

Self-Care Practices	Mon	Tue	Wed	Thu	Fri	Sat	Sun

SIMPLE WEIGHT TRACKER

DATE	TIME	WEIGHT	NOTES / COMMENTS

SIMPLE WEIGHT TRACKER

DATE	TIME	WEIGHT	NOTES / COMMENTS

SIMPLE WEIGHT TRACKER

DATE	TIME	WEIGHT	NOTES / COMMENTS

SIMPLE WEIGHT TRACKER

DATE	TIME	WEIGHT	NOTES / COMMENTS

DESTINATION

DATE

PLACES TO VISIT

TO DO

- [ ]
- [ ]
- [ ]
- [ ]
- [ ]
- [ ]
- [ ]

TRANSPORTATION

DEPARTURE	ARRIVAL

DEPARTURE	ARRIVAL

DEPARTURE	ARRIVAL

MONEY SPEND

ACCOMMODATION

NAME

BOOKING

ADDRESS

TEL. ROOM

NOTES

DESTINATION

DATE

PLACES TO VISIT

TO DO

- [ ]
- [ ]
- [ ]
- [ ]
- [ ]
- [ ]
- [ ]

TRANSPORTATION

DEPARTURE	ARRIVAL

DEPARTURE	ARRIVAL

DEPARTURE	ARRIVAL

ACCOMMODATION

NAME

BOOKING

ADDRESS

TEL. ROOM

NOTES

MONEY SPEND

DESTINATION

DATE

PLACES TO VISIT

TO DO

- [ ]
- [ ]
- [ ]
- [ ]
- [ ]
- [ ]
- [ ]

TRANSPORTATION

DEPARTURE	ARRIVAL

DEPARTURE	ARRIVAL

DEPARTURE	ARRIVAL

MONEY SPEND

ACCOMMODATION

NAME

BOOKING

ADDRESS

TEL.

ROOM

NOTES

- Acts of Kindness Tracker -

Kindness	Recipient	Completed

- Acts of Kindness Tracker -

Kindness	Recipient	Completed

- Acts of Kindness Tracker -

Kindness	Recipient	Completed

To-Do List

To-Do List

To-Do List

30 DAY CHALLENGE

CHALLENGE TYPE

NOTES

30 DAY CHALLENGE

CHALLENGE TYPE		1	2
3	4	5	6
7	8	9	10
11	12	13	14
15	16	17	18
19	20	21	22
23	24	25	26
27	28	29	30

NOTES

30 DAY CHALLENGE

CHALLENGE TYPE

NOTES

Easy Password Tracker

Site	Username	Password

Easy Password Tracker

Site	Username	Password

MILEAGE LOG

MAKE:		MODEL:		YEAR:
DATE:	ODOMETER: START | END		TOTAL:	DESTINATION / PURPOSE:

MILEAGE LOG

MAKE:		MODEL:		YEAR:
DATE:	**ODOMETER: START | END**		**TOTAL:**	**DESTINATION / PURPOSE:**

NOTES

NOTES

NOTES

Made in the USA
Monee, IL
04 November 2026

67375586R00056